A *Christian* Road Less Traveled

Seven Key Steps to Guide You On the Narrow Path to a Successful Christian Life

Buck Jacobs

The C12 Group, LLC

Copyright © 2016

Dedicated to the readers of this book in the hope that on the other side of the Bema judgment seat of Christ, you'll be glad you've read it.

Contents

Foreword

I am honored to introduce you to Buck Jacobs's new book, *A Christian Road Less Traveled.* From the day I met Buck, he has been a dear friend and trusted advisor. In fact, other than my own father, Buck is the most inspirational man to whom I can point as one who consistently lives out the Christian faith at work. I believe if there is ever a hall of fame for marketplace ministry leaders, Buck Jacobs would be one of the first selected. Of course, his personal humility would probably keep him from accepting such an award.

Buck's life has been a journey of overcoming the desire for praise of man to one of pursuing a life of discipleship and praising the name of his Lord and Savior, Jesus Christ. I know the only reward Buck truly desires is to hear his Savior say, "Well done, good and faithful servant."

Buck is a man of conviction. He won't tell you what you want to hear. Buck tells it like it is, yet he clearly speaks the truth in love. I recall on my fiftieth birthday when my wife, Robin, honored me by collecting and reading notes written to me from friends and business associates. Most of the messages were flattering and personally rewarding, while others commented on how I had impacted their lives. Robin and I joked that it might be a good idea to save these notes to read at my funeral. However, Buck's note was quite different. He highlighted some people through whom God did extraordinary things well beyond their fiftieth birthday. Then he reminded me it was after his own fiftieth birthday that God allowed him to start The C12 Group, which has since grown into the largest peer advisory network of Christian CEO's and business owners in North America. His note finished with "What you waiting for, kid? Get to work! God has much to accomplish through you in the years ahead." Buck wants all of us to relentlessly pursue God's purpose for our lives.

We could all use a mentor like Buck Jacobs in our life. That's why I am so excited that Buck has written this book. I am convinced that in reading *A Christian Road Less Traveled*, Buck will speak truth into your life just as he has continually spoken truth into mine. Enjoy the journey.

Kris DenBesten
CEO Vermeer Southeast
Author of *Shine, Gracyn's Song, Crisis Survival Guide*,
and *The Shine Factor*

Preface

What is success? How do you define it? How does Jesus define it? To be successful, even highly successful as a Christian, our definition must be the same as His. He is the One who will ultimately judge it. (2Corinthians 5:10) In the context of this book, the word "success" will ultimately be found when we come before Jesus and hear Him say, "Well done, good and faithful servant!" Christians can live in a way that might be judged as successful here on earth by the standards of this world, but will be seen as much less successful in heaven. How do you think Jesus will define success? What will His definition be? Would you care to be successful in the world's eyes and not in His? Our hope in writing this short book is to increase our understanding and awareness of this vital distinction, and to provide some practical tools to promote eternal success.

We are in a unique condition as we read this material, a condition that is temporary but significant—a condition that we shall experience only once in all of eternity. God chose to create us to be spirit beings temporarily inhabiting a human body. We will not always be as we are now. A day will come when each of us will end this life experience, and go on to another experience of life called eternal life. But, for the moment we are living in the human experience of life.

Because we are in reality living simultaneously in two dimensions of the same life, what the Bible calls temporal and eternal—one spiritual and one in the flesh—we can easily become distracted or confused. Since the life in the flesh is physical, visible, and connected to our natural senses, it appears to be more real to us and thus more important. This of course is not true. Eternal life is infinitely more important and our spiritual lives are more important than our physical ones.

We walk on this earth for a season, a season that has both a beginning and an end. We are now somewhere in between beginning and end, but exactly where we don't know. How we invest our lives matters, and the things we invest our lives in are born in the things we think about and the way we perceive them.

In an attempt to address what success is, how to define it, and most importantly how Jesus defines it, we've written seven "steps" that may help you grasp this important approach to a successful life. It is our hope these will help you live as true followers of Jesus Christ and lead others to do the same.

Before we discuss the first step, it might be helpful if we define several of our terms. First, the word "step" itself. What do you think of when you hear the word "step"? For most, it will mean a forward motion or effort, and will suggest a positive sense of the word. Others might define a step as something that is done regularly, as an intentional effort or exercise to move forward.

Second, we need to look at the terms, "successful" and "Christians." A Christian is by definition—or at least should be—a disciple of Jesus Christ. Being successful as a disciple is to follow the teachings, example, and the way of life of Jesus in a way that promotes and produces the results the Teacher encourages. A disciple is an extension of his or her teacher, an expression of the essence of the one he or she follows.

A successful disciple will be effective in promoting the values of his/her teacher. What does "effective" mean in this case? Effective may be compared to the word "efficient," to add light to our topic. Efficient means to accomplish something with minimum effort or maximum proficiency. It is to be able to do something "right."

Effectiveness is different than efficient, however. Effectiveness means to do what is right, the correct thing, the correct way, and to produce or effect the right result. It is doing the right thing.

An efficient Christian may spend his or her whole life doing wrong things very well, and with great ease and little effort. Most of what passes for normal Christian life today is efficient. Francis Chan, in his book, *Crazy Love: Overwhelmed by a Relentless God*, makes this point well. As he says, "Christians should not fear failure but [they should fear] succeeding at the wrong things."

An effective and successful Christian life produces fruit like the fruit Jesus produced and taught us to strive for … fruit that is not what the world might call it … and success that is not at all what the world will call success. Effective Christians will be heroes and heroines in heaven, but maybe not on earth. There is a different standard to measure effectiveness on earth than what Jesus will use in heaven.

Effective, fruitful Christians change the world around them. They, and we, are called to be light and salt. When light or salt is introduced into an environment, it is changed. It is no longer the same because of the presence of light or salt. We, as containers of the living God, are called to be agents of change. We are not here to just survive life on earth; we are here to participate in changing it forever. Sure, it is His power that will change it, but He has chosen to manifest His power through us.

Finally, the word, "highly." Highly effective people are leaders who exemplify to a higher degree the things essential in the context of their organization or group. Highly effective Christians will be those who live their lives in such a way as to enable them to hear the words most precious to every disciple of Jesus Christ: "Well done, faithful son or daughter. Enter into the joy prepared for you from the foundations of the earth!" They will not only hear it themselves, but will influence others to live to hear them as well.

The Bible references in this book are from the New King James version (NKJV) of the Bible.

May your thoughts and mine be encouraged to measure what we do and what we think in terms of the eternal significance they represent, and may we search for eternal success in our efforts together.

Buck Jacobs

Step 1: Accept Personal Responsibility

Old men sit by the fire, dozing and dreaming, not so much about what was, but about what might have been.—Anonymous

The term "proactive" means "to accept responsibility for action." The easiest way to understand the word "proactive" is to see it in contrast to its opposite, or antonym word, reactive. Proactive means to take responsibility for an action, while reactive means to wait until action happens and then to respond to it.

A reactive person is like a reed in the wind, bending whichever way the wind blows. A reactive person primarily responds to the circumstances of life, something we must all do to some extent. But a proactive person recognizes while there are some things in life we cannot control, our way in life, and ultimately our success, will be largely determined by how we deal with those things that we can control. A truly proactive person realizes that success in life, both in the natural and the eternal sense, comes through discerning those things we control, and taking responsibility to initiate positive actions in those areas.

Many things are important, and possible, and those may affect our lives. Things like the potential crash of the Japanese stock market or a successful terrorist attack. Should such an event occur, we would all be affected in a negative way. But the truth is while it is possible and could be devastating, there is absolutely nothing we can do about it. To spend time and thought on the possibility is wasteful, compared to investing the same effort in things that we can control. Proactive people realize this truth.

There are two types of things to be aware of. First, those things we are concerned about but have no control over or influence with, and second, those we are concerned about and have control over or influence with. To be proactive we must decide to concentrate our life effort in the second area, that which we can control or influence. We cannot, perhaps, choose our circumstances, but we can choose our responses to our circumstances.

In the spiritual sense, we don't "choose the race that is set before us." God chooses the race, and we can choose how we run the race. In this sense we even choose how we finish it. To illustrate, let's agree that God is a proactive person. That is, He has accepted responsibility to initiate every positive action needed to make possible every aspect of every facet of what we are created or designed to do. For example, in the matter of our salvation—which is the cornerstone of our relationship with Him—what is there left for God to do in order that any man might be saved? Anything? No, there is nothing more that God needs to do. He has initiated and completed all that is in His power to do. He has given His Son, and the sacrifice is complete. He has sent His Spirit to roam the face of this earth, to seek and to call every man. What, then, is left undone? By God, nothing is undone. But by man, there is one thing yet to do. Each man must accept his responsibility for positive action and accept the gift that God has offered. To offer is God's sole responsibility, but to reach out and accept it is man's responsibility.

Beyond salvation, for our life to be effective Christians, even highly effective Christians, is there anything God has yet to do in order for us to be all that He has called or designed us to be or do? In this short span of time between our new birth and going home to be with our Lord, is there anything that God has yet to do for us to be able to fulfill His plan for our eternal destiny? Is God in heaven busily at work making preparations to provide all we need to do, or be all He planned from the foundation of the earth? No. It is all done. The only unknown at this time is our response to what He has done. God is so proactive that He calls us to be so as well. He has provided all that we need, to be all that He wants, and now He calls on us to respond by being proactive too.

His Word is filled with examples of His call to you and me to be proactive. He makes many statements about Himself and His ways for our lives, and then He calls on us to act on them. Jesus said, "I am the way, the truth, and the life, and no one comes to the Father but through me." He also said, "Come to me all you who labor and are heavy laden." Tell me, who can "come" for me? No one can. I must choose to come or not to come for myself. You can exhort me, pray for me, even beg me, but in the end I must choose for myself. The offer is universal, but the response must be individual. I must accept the responsibility to initiate action. I must be proactive to receive what has been offered. God's hand is stretched out to me; now I must reach out and receive the gift He has offered.

Hundreds of other examples apply to the life we are called to live. Who can "Seek first the Kingdom of God" for me? Who can choose to "be anxious for nothing" except me? Who else but you or I can "set your mind on things above?" Can I ask someone else to "walk in the Spirit" and therefore "not carry out the desires of the flesh" for me? No! It is up to you and me to choose for ourselves to be proactive and do those things. God's provision is perfect and complete; all that is left is for us to accept pro-actively what He has made available to us.

An old saying in psychology applies to this discussion. It goes: "If it is to be, it is up to me." There is a great and sobering truth in this statement. God has already done all that is needed for me to be all He wants me to be. The rest is my part, my choice. The truth is that your relationship with God, and my own, are exactly what we have decided they will be. If it were left only up to Him and we didn't have to make choices, our relationships would be wonderful because He chose to do everything needed for it to be so. But we have been given the freedom to make choices, to agree or comply with His plan and His way in our lives, so He must supply all we need to be successful. If He commands us to love, and we choose to obey and ask Him to supply the love we need, will He not do it? He must, or He is not God. We need never worry that He will not accept His full measure of responsibility for provision. He will. Our decision is to be proactive in obeying His call, and when we do, all the power of heaven is released on our behalf.

The step of pro-activity is the foundation for all the others to follow. To accept responsibility for my part in my relationship with God is the first step in becoming effective in my service to Him. Too many of us wait until someone or something else acts on us, forcing God's will into our lives to move on in Him. It doesn't work that way. The stage is set, the provisions are all there. You and I are the players and the game is on!

I'll close this segment with a quote from Donald Gray Barnhouse:

"Let us live, then, in the light of eternity. If we do not, we are weighing the scales against our eternal welfare. We must understand that 'whatsoever a man soweth' must be taken in its widest meaning, and that every thought and intent of the heart will come under the scrutiny of the Lord at His coming. We can be sure that at the Judgment Seat of Christ there will be a marked difference between the Christian who has lived his life before the Lord, clearly discerning what was for the glory of God, and another Christian who was saved at a rescue mission at the end of a depraved and vicious life, or a nominal Christian saved on his deathbed after a life of self-pride, self-righteousness, self-love, and self-sufficiency. All will be in heaven, but the differences will be eternal. We may be sure that the consequences of our character will survive the grave and that we shall face those consequences at the Judgment Seat of Christ."

A judgment where there are truly no choices involved would be an unjust judgment. That means if you and I have no options, no choices to make in doing the will of God, He would be unjust to judge our acts and actions. Being proactive is to make choices: to initiate action or to choose action. Being positively proactive is to make choices in the area of things that we can control that will produce a positive result. Our eternity will largely be the result of our proactive choices.

On Your Own

1. Define the word "proactive" in your own terms.

_____

_____

2. Pray, think about, and list any areas in your life that you are responsible for where you are being reactive, but know you should be proactive.

_____

_____

3. Take each item on your list and write a plan to change reaction to pro-action.

_____

_____

Step 2: Consider the Bema!

A journey of a thousand miles begins with one step, unless, of course, that step is in the wrong direction. In which case a much longer journey begins.—Anonymous

We'll open this segment with an analogy from Rick Warren's *The Purpose Driven Life: What on Earth Am I Here For?* Imagine yourself driving in your car one morning. It is about 10:00 AM and you are wearing your best suit or dress. It's a beautiful day and you are on your way to ... you're not sure. You find yourself turning into a neat and well-kept but rather formal-looking building. You're surprised to see it is a funeral home. You were not aware you would visit one today and wonder why you would be there.

Entering the door, you are directed to a viewing room on the left. As you walk in you see people you know, most of them quite well. There is a group from work in one corner, one from your neighborhood in another, and in still another, your church friends, and finally family ... lots of family.

Before you stop to speak to the others, your curiosity draws you to the casket to see who they are here to honor. You look into the casket and, to your amazement, it is you! You are at your own funeral. All the others, those who love and know you best, are there to say farewell to you, their friend, associate, neighbor, husband, or father.

Dear reader, use your imagination to ask yourself: If this were your funeral and the people who were there would speak truthfully, what would you want them to say about you? In the depth of your heart, what would you want those who know you best and love you most, to say about you at the point when it's too late to change anything … when all they can do is reflect on what you have shown them.

As you look around the crowd, is there one whom you have wounded and are not reconciled with? What would they say? It is now too late to ask for forgiveness or to make amends.

Are there any you have cheated or lied to? If so, it's too late to set it right. At this point, what's done is done. It is too late to tell anyone you love them or to thank them for loving you. The time is past when broken relationships could have been healed.

You would want your neighbors to say, "He was a great neighbor, always helpful, and we knew we could always rely on him for a good word or a helping hand." What would your neighbors be able to say today?

You would want your business associates to say, "He was a fine example of a Christian business person. His integrity was my model, and his loving way of dealing with people in tough situations taught me so much! He showed me that people count more than money." What would your business associates be saying at your funeral today, if they were being totally honest?

What would you want your friends from church to say? Something like, "He was the best brother I ever had in the Lord. He encouraged me to be all I can be in Christ and his example of placing Jesus first in his life taught and inspired me."

Now look and your wife and children. When it's all over and you can't change a thing, what do you want them to say? "He was a great dad … he showed he loved me in so many ways! We did so many things together because we're so special. I'll miss him so much! If he taught me anything, he taught me we won't be apart for long. I'll see him again, and I can't wait to thank him for being the dad he was." Or, "He was my best friend, my lover, and my inspiration in Christ. No woman was more blessed than I to live with a godly and loving husband. He always put me first, made me feel so special. He modeled Jesus to me more than anyone I know."

Are these the kinds of things you want those who know you best and love you most to say about you? Who wouldn't? Well, it is in your power and mine to make it so, but we must begin today.

We create our own legacy. We write our own epitaph. If we want to be remembered as loving and kind, we must live as a loving and kind person day by day. If we desire to be remembered as honest, we must live honestly each day.

Too many of us think we can do things at the end of our lives that will enhance our legacy, like endowing a fund to do good works or leaving a large sum to a charity. The truth is: Our heritage becomes established by the little things we do every day, through our habits and our disciplines. Money left to a good work earned from a lifetime of worldly or compromised living (James 4:17) will not change the record. Witness the legacy of the "rich man" Jesus spoke of in Luke 12:15-21. He had a great year, a big business, and decided to expand his wealth. But what is he remembered for? He will be remembered as the man God called a "fool." When his name is mentioned, what is remembered about him? Successful entrepreneur? Builder or great businesses? No! He will forever be known as the fool who laid up treasure for himself, but was not rich toward God. He built his heritage while he lived.

You and I are what we do every day, minute by minute. Our values are exposed by our actions, our priorities shown by our deeds. If we would live our lives in such a way as to allow those who know us and love us to give a good report of our lives, we must have a "true north" that will guide us day by day. We must begin, and live, with that end in mind. Everything is important for our ending. To finish well, we must begin well, and that requires knowing where we are going.

What have these statements and assertions brought to your mind? How do you feel as you read and/or listen to these things? If you are like the vast majority, you most likely feel convicted.

Most of us live our lives in the tyranny of the urgent. And because we have no particular end in mind other than some ill-defined idea that it will come someday, we flounder in a sea of distraction. We struggle in the quicksand of the mundane, never setting a true course guided by an end we establish as supremely worthy.

To begin with the end in mind requires vision and goals for our life ... personal vision and goals. A favorite definition of vision is: "a perceived worthy result." Scripture confirms, "Without vision, a people perish." (Proverbs 29:18) To be guided in our daily habits and discipline we need to know where it is we want to arrive, to know what Stephen R. Covey calls our "true north." What he calls true north is our ultimate purpose.

As we have discussed, the reports by those who know us and love us at the end of our lives have stirred us emotionally. That is a normal, healthy reaction to the exercise. We all want those we know and love to think well of us at the end of our days on earth. But for Christians, that is not the end of the story; in fact, it is not even the most important part of the story. For Christians there is a more important dimension, the eternal dimension. There is a judgment even more important than that of those who know us and love us here. It is the reputation with, and judgment of, He who truly knows us best and loves us most: Jesus Christ.

To frame this discussion we'll look at three key Scripture verses. We'll read them first and comment afterward. First, Romans 14:10b says, "For we shall ALL stand before the judgment seat of Christ." Verse 12 of the same chapter reads, "So then EACH of us shall give account of himself to God." Next, 2 Corinthians 5:10 follows: "For we must ALL appear before the judgment seat of Christ, that EACH ONE may receive the things done in the body, according to what he has done, whether good or bad." The key passage is found in 1 Corinthians 3:11–15: "For no other foundation can ANYONE lay than that which is laid, which is Jesus Christ. Now if ANYONE builds on this foundation with gold, silver, precious stones, wood, hay, straw, EACH ONE'S work will become manifest; for the Day will declare it, because it will be revealed by fire; and the fire will test EACH ONE'S work, of what sort of work it is. If ANYONE'S work which he has built on it endures, he will receive a reward. If ANYONE'S work is burned he will suffer loss; but he himself will be saved yet so as through fire."

These Scriptures describe and promise what is called the "Bema" seat of Christ, or the judgment seat of Christ. It is the place of final accounting for each Christian. The Scripture says we have no foundation except Jesus Christ. We receive this foundation when we ask Him to forgive our sins, and promise to follow Him as He takes up residence in our hearts in the form of His Holy Spirit. We thus enter into the plan that God has had in His heart for us from the time before He made the world. Ephesians 2:10 states: "For we are His workmanship, created in Christ Jesus for good works, which God prepared beforehand that we should walk in them." We are not saved by good works but we are saved to do good works.

We walk on this earth for a season when EACH of us has a part God has designed for us to play in His eternal plan. We are given His name as sons and daughters, and the title of Ambassador of Reconciliation. He lives in us, and attempts to live through us during this season. At some point our assignment ends and we are called back home to be with Him. Before entering into the place He has prepared for us, we must EACH pass through the Bema seat. As we do, the judgment will be between Him and us alone. We will not pass through with our spouse, pastors, or friends. It will be just you or me and Jesus. Never doubt this fact: We are inexorably progressing toward the Bema seat day by day, minute by minute, tick by tick. NO ONE will enter heaven except through this place.

What will the criteria be? What is He looking for in our lives? Is it possible to know now? The answers to these questions are not fully known, but there is plenty of evidence to the general nature of the key issues. One thing is for sure: In eternal terms, nothing is more important to us than a right understanding of this topic. Whatever we gain on earth we will leave behind, and whatever we have sent ahead will be waiting for us. What is it that we can send ahead? It will probably seem like a simplistic answer, but in your writer's opinion there is only one thing which matters: obedience. Obedience in following Him and His will in the life He created us to live. This obedience will manifest itself in various ways, and they will all be the result of obedience to Him and His plan for our earthly service to Him.

It won't matter if we finish our race with a great big pile of stuff or even a little pile. It won't matter if the whole world thinks we have been the greatest person or the greatest fool. It won't matter if we have been recognized as godly or rejected as radical freaks. It will only matter that we have been what He designed, and have done what He asked. He will supply all we need to be and do for all He asks. The only missing ingredient is our obedience.

What about your funeral? The reality is it doesn't even matter what anyone says at our funeral. People can be wrong, but Jesus is always right. The only worthy end to which a Christian should aspire is to appear before the Bema judgment and hear, "Well done, good and faithful servant!"

Christians must focus on the real end. Our funerals are not the end of anything except our brief stint of service on a fallen planet. We go on into an eternity that is as fully promised to be influenced by our works on earth as it is promised to exist at all. Our judgment is as sure as our salvation. We are not here to merely survive—we are here to serve and to be rewarded for our service.

This being true, how then shall we live? We must live with this end in mind. First, determine what we want the end to be, and then proactively focus our life with all our strength and will on the things we can control to achieve it. There is no other reasonable conclusion. "A man IS NO FOOL who gives up what HE CANNOT KEEP, to get what HE CANNOT LOSE!" All of the riches of this world will be lost to their owner's use one day. No one can carry a dime or a document into heaven: naked we come into this life and naked we leave it. Only what we have invested in the values of heaven will be of value to us in heaven. Our goal must set and drive the course of our lives. Once we know the end, we can properly plan the way.

Once we determine what end we seek, developing a personal mission statement will become extremely helpful. Even as our businesses benefit from having a clear mission statement, so much more will our lives. The characteristics of a personal mission statement are the same as those of a corporate statement. It must be clear, short, inspirational, and helpful for making decisions to successfully function under its guidance ... a functional arbiter, if you will.

For your worksheet on this chapter, begin to articulate your personal mission statement.

On Your Own

The "end" that I have in mind for my life is:

_____

_____

_____

_____

The things that I must do to accomplish that "end" are:

a. _____

b. _____

c. _____

d. _____

Things I must change to accomplish that "end" are:

a. _____

b. _____

c. _____

d. _____

Step 3: Nurture Your Priorities

Things which matter most must never be at the mercy of things which matter least.—Goethe

Before we begin Step 3, let's review Steps 1 and 2. Truly, without a genuine grasp of the first two steps, applying the Nurture Your Priorities step (and purpose-centered living itself) is impossible.

Step 1 told us to accept personal responsibility. That is, to accept our responsibility for acting in a positive way in those areas of life we have control over or can influence. We determine our spiritual destiny based on our choices. God has made everything available to us for all that He wants us to be. We must simply choose to believe it and act on our belief.

Step 2 said once we understand we are responsible for initiating positive action, we need to have a "true north" destination, or goal, so we can "Consider the Bema." Our goal was defined by what we want more than anything else to accomplish with our lives. What we want most will define what we focus on and invest in, and will have a huge influence on the rewards we may receive in the world to come. We said for Christians, this would be measured by Jesus at the Bema judgment seat, and our primary goal in life should be to hear him say, "Well done!" at its end. Step 2 basically said we need to look at this life with eternity in mind and decide now to strive for those things which have the most eternal significance.

In these terms, we see that all the things we choose to do or use in our lives have a relative worth. Some are eternal and are therefore worth a good deal more than others which have value only in this short life on earth. The ultimate measure of success for our lives will be the sum total of what we have done day by day that has eternal value. So, to be truly successful, we must begin to do on a daily basis those things that will add up to what we perceive to be our chosen endgame. Doing so requires a strong and continuous commitment. Now, on to Step 3, "Nurture Your Priorities."

The quote we used at the start of the segment says: "Things which matter most must never be at the mercy of things that matter least." That's what nurturing our priorities is all about. Our priorities are those things that are most important in attaining our "endgame," as God defines it.

The most important things in a successful life are a combination of big and little things—priorities that feed into our goals and objectives. First things are first, and should be more important than the other, smaller things. The importance of all things is how they effect, and affect, our endgame. Achieving our goals requires our emphasis on those things that feed it best, and a de-emphasis or elimination of those that do not.

In business management, there is a theory called Pareto's law, or the Pareto principle. Pareto asserts that we get 80 percent of our desired results from 20 percent of our efforts. Other applications are that we get 80 percent of our profits from 20 percent of our customers, 80 percent of our good work from 20 percent of our employees, or in church ... 80 percent of the giving comes from 20 percent of the people. In terms of our life goals, there is a relationship there as well. In the totality of our lives we'll probably get 80 percent of our spiritual rewards from the things we do with 20 percent of our time. It comes down to what we do with what God gave us.

We all have different gifts and talents. Some have higher intelligence than others, while some are quicker thinkers. Some may be physically stronger, and so on. We are different ages, and have access to different amounts of resources and different levels of opportunity. We are as alike as snowflakes; that is to say, not alike at all. We are individuals created to be different from each other, by a God who knew exactly what He was doing. We are somewhat alike in some ways but mostly different, very different.

Yet there is one thing we all have in common: time. Each day we all get 24 hours. No one gets more or less time, but there may be a great difference in how that time is spent or invested.

As it relates to the Pareto principle, there is a large portion of our daily 24 hours that we really have little control over. God made us to need food, to sleep, and to work. Things happen to us which we can't control, such as storms, illnesses, and so on. We all have functional responsibilities such as driving to work, traveling for business, cutting the grass, and caring for our bodies through diet and exercise. Sometimes, emergencies demand immediate attention, like a phone call from an angry customer, or a hurting friend. When we look at it, Pareto was right: we probably have about 20 percent of our 24 hours on a daily basis available to gain 80 percent of our endgame.

These aren't absolute numbers, of course, but the point is how little time we have to make choices about how we will affect our end. Reactive people let others, or circumstances, eat up the 20 percent of their truly valuable time. Proactive people don't let that happen. Proactive people make value judgments on the use of their time because they recognize that unless they control the things they can control, they will be controlled by them.

Time is the one nonrenewable resource we all receive in equal amounts from God every day. He gives it to us and allows us to decide how we will use it. Never be deceived; we do make decisions, and we are accountable for how we make them. No one can force us to do anything. Ultimately, we choose to do everything we do. To think otherwise is a cop-out with eternal ramifications. You and I don't have to be doing what we are doing, even at this very moment. Even in the most extreme situations, no one can force us to do anything we don't want to do or don't believe in. We can choose to die first. Throughout history, many have.

There is no way to overemphasize the consequences of our choices. How and for what we invest the time we have is primary on our list of things we need to consider carefully. "Only one life, soon to be past, only what's done for Christ will last" is not simplistic jargon. It is the reality of our lives as Christians.

Steven R. Covey describes a wonderful tool in two of his books, *The 7 Habits of Highly Effective People* and *First Things First*, which we can use to great benefit. I will outline a simple version of it here. If after applying the simple version you realize sufficient gain, you can get more details from reading his books.

To begin, take a plain sheet of paper and draw a line down the middle, from top to bottom of the page. Next, draw another line from side to side, again through the middle. You will have created a matrix with four equal quadrants. Call the top left Quadrant #1, the top right #2, the lower left #3, and the lower right #4.

1. Important - Urgent.	2. Important - Not Urgent
3. Not Important - Urgent	4. Not Important - Not Urgent

Now, in the daily mix of events we contend with or choose to spend time on, there are basically two kinds of things which we do: those that are important and those that are not important. Write the word "Important" to the left of Quadrant #1 and "Not Important" to the left of Quadrant #3.

For our purposes here, there are only two definitions for the things we do when we can or must do them. They are either urgent or not urgent. Write the words "Urgent" over Quadrant #1 and "Not Urgent" over Quadrant #2.

We now have four quadrants: Urgent and Important (#1), Not Urgent but Important (#2), Urgent but Not Important (#3), and Not Urgent and Not Important (#4).

All the activities of our lives may be assigned to one of these four designations. Keep in mind our definition of important as "that which feeds those things that we care most about."

Now let's look at some things that would be classified as both urgent and important for your Quadrant #1. They might be crises of various kinds, pressing problems, deadline-driven projects, or emergencies. An emergency could be a sudden illness or a natural disaster—things we have no control over and must deal with immediately. Other kinds of emergencies could be agreeing to a deadline, which gains urgency as the deadline approaches. Other problems may be pressed upon us by others and we're not able to avoid them. Quadrant #1 activities are genuinely urgent and important. Think of some examples in your life.

Quadrant #2 is for activities that are not urgent but important. These are usually flexible. Examples would be health maintenance, relationship building, planning, rest, recreation, hobbies, and study of important materials. Other examples are working out three to four times per week (important indeed, yet flexible as to when it is done), writing a family mission statement, providing for adequate sleep, strategic planning, or just sitting quietly and thinking about God, family, life, or whatever. We can pretty much do these things anytime, yet they are still important.

Quadrant #3 consists of things that are urgent but not important. Examples are going to the movies, watching a ball game, random interruptions, phone calls, meetings, or other time-driven events of little significance. Answering the phone to speak to telemarketers is a great example of a Quadrant #3 activity. It is urgent because it happens right now, but it is not important.

Quadrant #4 is filled with the things we do that are not urgent or important. They are the time wasters of our lives. Some examples are busy work like junk mail and junk food—not good for much, but filler-uppers of our lives nevertheless. Other things, like watching most of what's on TV, keeping up with Facebook or Twitter, and going to most movies ... do nothing to feed our End. They merely devour our time—time, the one thing we really can't afford to waste. The worst message in Quadrant #4 is the time we waste: it is a large proportion of what we call "discretionary time." Discretionary time is the time we have the most freedom to choose in how we spend or invest it. It is time we have not promised to someone else, and it is not affected by other priorities. It is free to be used the way we choose.

These are the four basic divisions. Now, which of the four do you suppose has the greatest potential for feeding our End? Certainly not #3 or #4. We have shown they were made up of things that are urgent but not important, and not urgent and not important.

The greatest benefit must come from #1 and/or #2. We have said they are both important, but what is the primary difference between the two? The difference is in Quadrant #1 where we are mostly reacting to things that are urgent and important, but in Quadrant #2 we are primarily proactive. It is in the Quadrant #2 activities that we take control of our lives. We make our plans, do our thinking, and create our strategies in Quadrant #2. Taking control of our lives and nurturing our priorities are also done in Quadrant #2.

Here is a simple way to capture the benefit of this exercise. First, make a Quadrant #2 decision to set aside just one hour on Sunday nights for a Quadrant #2 activity. You will probably have to steal the time from #3 or #4 to do this, but you'll have the rest of Sunday night to do them. Just set aside one hour.

During this hour, make a list of things that are the most important, that feed the priorities you want to accomplish with your life. Write them on a sheet of paper or a legal pad. Then break them down into increments of hours or parts of hours. For example, if you want to spend an hour a day in Bible study, prayer, and fellowship with God, or take your wife on a date each week, write that down. If you think spending two hours per week with each child in an activity that they choose is important, write that down. Maybe you want to read a trade magazine for 30 minutes per day or exercise for one hour four times per week. Write it down. Don't put your brain on overload; simply list four or five things that will feed your endgame, which you are either not doing or not doing consistently. Commit to pray about these things for the next week.

If you don't already have one, get a monthly planner with weekly and daily planning capability, or set up your digital calendar with the days broken down in hourly increments.

The following Sunday night, spend the first half of an hour in Quadrant #2 to review the list from the first week. If God has shown you other items that should be on it, add them. If He has shown you others that should not be there, take them off. Try to settle on no more than five basic important things.

The second half of the hour, use your calendar to make appointments for the time you will use for each item for the following week. Commit to use your calendar each day, booking your other commitments around the priority appointments you have identified and scheduled in advance. Some may be set up as recurring appointments and automatically booked each week, such as daily quiet time or weekly date nights with your spouse or children.

Do this every Sunday night. You will find that as simple as it is, you will begin to truly nurture the priorities in your life. If you do this for the rest of the time that God allows you on earth, you will be one happy camper in heaven!

Again, what I've described is found in Stephen R. Covey's books. You can read them if you want, but at the end of the day it all comes down to what I have just shared: first, deciding on goals or objectives that we care about most, and then committing the time to consistently engage with and nurture them. No system will work unless we work it. A simple system with a large commitment will be far more successful than an expensive and complicated one with little commitment. It is our choice. God knows what is most important to us, but He will not make our choices for us. We must decide to accept personal responsibility. We must decide what our endgame will be. We must consider the Bema, and then we, and only we, must commit to nurture our priorities. God will always be there to help, but the first move will be ours.

On Your Own

1. Next Sunday night, try the exercise suggested in our segment.

2. The next week, do it again.

3. And again.

4. And one more time.

5. Write and tell us how doing it affected your effectiveness.

Step 4: Practice Win-Win—Living and Leading

"I will always have all I need to do all God asks." Anon

The first three steps dealt with how we discipline ourselves and the way we deal with our inner selves and how we establish our ultimate goals and priorities. Now we will look at the next three steps, which refer to our ability to deal effectively with others as Christ-centered servant leaders. For most of us, learning to deal with others in a way that is win-win goes against what we have been taught and against our very nature as well.

Success as a disciple depends on our effectiveness in leading others in their pursuit of Kingdom principles and values, just as Jesus did. Real leaders are those who have volunteer followers, so our success as leaders depends on our ability to encourage others to voluntarily engage in our plan, project, or mission. No one succeeds alone. If we are going to be considered highly effective Christians, it will be largely due to how we relate with others and positively influence them for Christ.

As we approach this topic, we should identify possible examples of interactions we might use in our approach to relationships. There are six.

First, we could choose to approach relationships on a win-win basis. This paradigm strives for mutual benefit. It says that what we do together must be as good for you as it is for me. A form of win-

win, called "win-win or no deal," is what we will end up advocating as the only real, effective way to deal with others in the longterm. Dealing with others from the win-win or no deal paradigm says, "As a Christian business person, I am committed to dealing with you in a way that assures that you will benefit as much as me, and if that is not possible, I won't deal at all. I will not take advantage of you in any way." Later on, we'll address that further.

There is a serious twofold problem with the win-win model. The first part of the problem is our fallen nature, which is selfish at its base. History records clearly that left on his own, man will serve himself to his advantage and hurt others if he perceives it as necessary to gain his ends. The second part of the problem is the way of the world, which is based on a faulted understanding of God's economy.

These two combine to form the most common paradigm, or attitude we hold as we approach relating to others, called "win-lose." It says that in order for me to get all that I want or need, someone else has to give up something they want or need. This paradigm is based on understanding life as a zero-sum game, that there are only so many goodies to go around, and if I gain any, someone else can't have them. Win-lose presumes an economy of scarcity, that everything that is good is in limited supply, and to gain it I must take it away from someone else. Dealing with people based on this model leads to manipulation rather than mutual benefit in a relationship.

Most businesses are managed and run primarily with a win-lose paradigm. Leaders try to take advantage of workers, and workers fight back, each attempting to manipulate the other into a subordinate or losing position. In the long term, working with the win-lose paradigm ends up in the third possible paradigm, although no sane person believes it to be desirable. This is called "lose-lose." In lose-lose relationships, no one wins. Everyone loses. Lose-lose relationships are sick and unhealthy, and only those with unhealthy minds would intentionally pursue them, although some do.

A fourth possible category is "lose-win," when one intends to lose so that the other may win. At first this might sound like a highly spiritual paradigm, but it is not. It is an arrangement that cannot be sustained. The loser will never be encouraged to continue in a lose-win relationship. And while there may be times when one will give up something voluntarily so the other may be helped, this act of giving will not sustain a relationship. Even in the ultimate example where it appeared that Jesus had lost so that we might gain, we see that in reality His act was, and is, win-win. (Hebrews 12:2)

Some will play with the fifth paradigm called "win only." They don't care what happens to others as long as they get what they want. These are the sad losers who see all of life as a competition and every situation or relationship as a game to be won or lost. As one saying goes, "Winning isn't the important thing, it's the only thing." This is the typical hedonistic, self-concerned attitude we see often in our society today. The problem is no one can win all the time, and when that reality sets in, all sorts of trauma happens to those practicing win only—and to those around them.

Considering these five paradigms, we may all find ourselves in situations where we function in one or more of the less desirable categories for emergency or short-term purposes. For instance, there may be times when we use lose-win to preserve a relationship when the issue isn't worth fighting over. Or we might move out of win only if our child's life were in danger. But our discussion is not about the exception to the rule. We are looking at what our paradigm should be for the long run ... to gain and maintain effective influence with other people. That means operating in an interdependent relationship where we mutually receive and give throughout the process. When this is the case, win-win is the only effective option, and the highest form of win-win is called "win-win or no deal." That is our sixth and final possible paradigm of interaction. And because we are not naturally drawn to operate in this paradigm which says unless we can come to a place where we benefit to our mutual satisfaction or we won't proceed, we must learn to think in a different way or change our paradigm. To operate out of the win-win or no deal paradigm is the most effective way to influence others for the long term.

To begin to create the framework for this paradigm, we must first understand the faulted basis of the world's view of the "goodies." As we stated earlier, the "world" (meaning those outside of God's Kingdom or those who are in it but don't understand it) believes in what is called an economy of scarcity. An economy of scarcity is the concept of limited resources: that there is only so much of whatever to go around. In the economy of scarcity, whatever I gain is taken out of the game and no one else can have it. It is also called a zero-sum game. People who are locked into believing in an economy of scarcity don't believe in God's sovereign ability to provide. This is a critical problem when it occurs in Christians.

The fact is that God is not limited in any way. He is the Creator. If he needs more of anything, it is available to Him at any time. That means a man or a woman walking with God walks in a constant economy of abundance. There is never a lack of whatever is needed to do anything God wants done! As it has often been said, "God's will done God's way, will never lack God's resources." Think about it. What would it say about God if He asked you or me to do something and couldn't supply whatever we needed to do it? In fact, in paradoxical contrast to the world's false concept, Jesus teaches us that to gain we MUST give, and to lead we MUST serve. There is always enough to do anything God wants done in our lives, in our relationships with others, and in our relationship with Him. We truly live in the midst of the greatest economy of abundance imaginable. We never have to think win-lose. No one needs to give up anything in order for us to have, and be all that God intends for us.

It is in this context that Philippians 2:3–4 becomes not only possible, but desirable. "Let nothing be done through selfish ambition or conceit, but in lowliness of mind let each esteem others as better than himself. Let each of you look out not only for his own interests, but also for the interests of others." This is win-win thinking, and so is the Golden Rule: "And just as you want men to do to you, do also to them likewise." (Luke 6:31 and Matthew 7:12)

The first step in developing the win-win or no deal paradigm is to rightly perceive ourselves and our relationship to God and His Kingdom. We are not animals seeking sustenance from a limited game pool, nor are we heathens striving to gain as much of this world's wealth as possible, believing this is as close to heaven as we will ever get. No, a thousand times no! We are not created that way—unless we choose to see ourselves as such.

Complete the following to learn who God says we are.

1. John 1:12 – I am a _____ of _____.
2. Romans 8:17 – I am a _____ _____ with _____.
3. 2 Corinthians 5:20 – I am an _____ for _____.
4. 1 Peter 2:11 – I am a _____ and _____.

This short Bible study tells us the reality of our identity in Christ. This is not "pie in the sky for the great by and by." It is who we really are now.

To reiterate, we are: (1) a son or a daughter of the Most High God, (2) a joint heir with His only begotten and most loved Son, Jesus, appointed as (3) His Ambassador of Reconciliation as I pass through this world as a (4) sojourner and pilgrim, I shall never lack His resources.

God is not a cruel Father who asks us to do things but refuses to provide what we need to do them; He is the King of Kings who commands all things to be available to those who walk with Him, and gives good gifts to all who serve Him.

So I ask you: Need we ever be concerned that we must take from anyone else to have all we need? Does anyone else have to lose so that we can win? And if we walk with Him, can we ever lose? No! The world is limited, but the Kingdom of God is infinite. God's resources are infinite.

Learning to think win-win is a fundamental requirement for effective Christian leadership. Leaders who think and act out of a win-lose paradigm are not really leaders, they're manipulators attempting to use others to gain their own selfish ends. This style may work short term in some situations, but it fails in the end. True Christian leadership is longterm ... very long-term.

Jesus said, "I am among you as one who serves." Our long-term gain in the Kingdom of God will be measured by our obedience and our service. Ministry in, and through, our business requires that we love and serve others through the daily vicissitudes of doing business (or life, for that matter). If we enter the process with a commitment to win-win or no deal, based on a genuine belief in the truth of God's sovereign sufficiency, we will dramatically enhance our effectiveness.

Let's turn the Golden Rule upon ourselves for a moment. If you could select a leader to follow, which of the paradigms we have discussed would you pick for that leader? By considering the paradigms previously discussed, the choice is obvious, isn't it? Of course we would all choose to be led by a person committed to the paradigm of win-win or no deal. Why would we expect others to choose differently? Based on this example, it is obvious which paradigm we should strive for in our own leadership perspective.

Ministry—effective ministry—takes place through relationships. Our effectiveness in ministry, our business, and our lives will be determined largely by the quality of the relationships we build within them. The healthier and stronger our relationships, the more effective our ministry will be. Our Father is a relational God, and all of His commandments and principles are intended to produce healthy relationships between Him and man, and between man and man. Relationships with a commitment to win-win or no deal have the highest chance of producing eternal fruit.

On Your Own

1. Examine the key relationships you have with your:

spouse   key employees

children   key suppliers

neighbors   key customers

friends   competitors

2. Ask yourself this question regarding your relationship with each of the above: "What paradigm am I using as I look at each of these people?"

3. If any of your answers were less than win-win or no deal, ask yourself: "What could I change to make it win-win or no deal? What things are in my control that could create win-win or no deal?"

4. Are you willing to make the changes you identify? Ask yourself why or why not.

Step 5: Practice EMBER

More dear in the sight of God and His angels than any other conquest is the conquest of self.—Arthur P. Stanley

If you were to ask the question, "Who wrote the book, *How to Win Friends with Influential People?*" to ten people, probably eight or nine would answer, "Dale Carnegie." You yourself might even give that answer. Unfortunately, it is the wrong answer. Dale Carnegie wrote the book, *How to Win Friends and Influence People*, not *How to Win Friends with Influential People*. This illustrates a problem with communication because no one really listens well. At least, only a few listen well. What passes for communication in most relationships today is not two-way communication, but two one-way communications happening at the same time. Most of us are more concerned with what we hope to say to another and wait for a chance to make our own points, than we are about understanding what they are trying to tell us. Even if we don't actually feel that way, our actions indicate that what we have to say is much more important than what might be coming our way.

A common and unfortunate example of this is seen on many Sunday mornings in our local churches. Have you noticed when you try to talk with some leaders that they seldom make eye contact with you? They might look over your shoulder or roam through the crowd looking for someone more important to talk with. Or so it seems.

More than once, your writer has had someone walk away in mid-sentence, saying, "Excuse me, I just have to …."

In one instance I decided to test the depth of such maladjustment. In response to the perfunctory "How are you?" extended by an elder in the church I attended as we shook hands and hugged one Sunday morning, I replied, "Not so good. I just found out I have cancer and only a few months to live." Without batting an eye he said, "That's good. Praise the Lord," as he moved by me to speak with another elder. The man who did this was, and is, a friend. He meant no harm or disrespect; he just didn't place a high enough value on the conversation to focus on hearing what was actually being said. Since he knew me and thought he knew my circumstances, he assumed everything was all right and he had no need to honestly inquire. As I said, he is still a friend, but truth be told, I have never been as able to fully trust him from that day. Nor am I fully able to trust other leaders within the church, or without, who practice selective listening in this way. Their effectiveness with me has been diminished by some degree.

What is your experience? Am I alone in this? I'm sure I'm not, and I'm also sure that this practice in leadership detracts from their effectiveness.

We all want to be treated with respect as individuals. One of the greatest forms of respect is listening to another person with the purpose of understanding what they say. If we move away from this practice, we lose effectiveness. When we give others the signal that what they have to say is not very important to us, they will remove themselves from us emotionally. One cause of the problem is mechanical and the other is psychological. Both can be dealt with successfully.

First, the mechanical. The problem stems from the fact that we all think much faster than we talk … unless, of course, we are from New York. Everyone from New York talks faster than anyone can think! Not really, though. In reality the average person thinks at a rate of up to 3,000 words per minute, but the average rate of speech is about

180 to 200 words per minute. This differential allows our minds to wander easily and promotes the second half of the deadly duo, which is psychological or even spiritual. Our common human need to be seen as "right" and our insecurity is heightened if another gets "first place" in something we are involved in, such as a conversation. It takes a secure person to be a good listener. Since we are all secure in Christ, as Christians, we have the ability to overcome this weakness if we work at it with His help.

There are two simple drills, or instruments, we can use to increase our abilities to listen and understand. Each is represented by an acronym to make them easy to remember.

The first, which deals with the mechanical side of the equation, is called EARS, which I'll explain shortly. EARS attempts to utilize the differential of our thinking and speaking rates in a positive way. Since we know ahead of time that people we speak with will talk far more slowly than we can think, we will use the differential for our mutual advantage. We will focus on hearing and understanding what is being said, by doing the four exercises of the acronym while the other person is speaking. Here's how it goes.

E stands for Evaluate. It means while the other person is speaking, I will focus on evaluating what they are saying by asking myself questions like, "Is this true to my knowledge?" Or "What are the sources for this information?" And "Is this something I need to hear?" We should spend part of the time listening in this mode, but we won't stay there.

We also utilize the **A** mode, which stands for Anticipate. In this, we ask ourselves, "Where is he/she going with this?" Or "What is going to be asked of me?" And "What is the point of this information in the eyes of this person?"

While the other is speaking, we may need to focus our attention to the **R** mode, which stands for Review. In Review, we mentally go back to the beginning of the conversation and review its content. We ask ourselves, "Where did we start this topic from?" Or "What did he/she say first about this?" And "When I said such and such, what was the response?"

If there is time, as in a more lengthy conversation, we can use the fourth mode, **S**, which means Speculate. This should be used sparingly, especially at first, because it can easily lapse into a distraction, like chasing rabbits. The S is normally not as helpful as E, A, and R, but with S we ask ourselves, "Why are they telling us this?" Or "What do they want me to do with this?" And "Who else needs to know this?"

If we commit to practice EARS, we will absolutely become better listeners. EARS is a simple focus tool that enables us to pay attention to what the other person is saying, rather than thinking about what we may want to say.

The second tool we'll discuss is another acronym: EMBER. It is a little more complicated, but will help us deal with the second, psychological, part of the listening problem. Using EMBER effectively requires most of us to apply a basic paradigm shift. The shift has a strong biblical perspective, with many examples. Romans 12:10 says to, "… give preference to one another." Philippians 2:3–4 stresses, "Let nothing be done through selfish ambition or conceit, but in lowliness of mind let each esteem others better than him. Let each of you look out not only for his own interests, but also for the interests of others." Then Romans 14:19 tells us, "Therefore let us pursue the things which make for peace and the things by which one may edify [or build up] another." Numerous other biblical exhortations instruct us to put the needs of others on at least as high a priority as our own, if not higher.

One more word before we delve into EMBER. In order for us to operate in the spirit of EMBER, we need to put ourselves in a biblical, Christlike mindset. The world usually bases its relationships on selfish criteria, namely, "What's in this for me?" We as Christians are called to use a different basis, when self is to be denied and others considered as objects of service, not objects to be manipulated for personal gain. EMBER captures the essence of this concept, and fits very well within the context of our seven key steps. I first encountered EMBER in a sales training class taught by Larry Wilson* years ago called "Relational Selling," and have used it ever since. See if you can hear echoes of biblical principles as well as some of our seven steps already discussed as we outline each letter.

E stands for Establishing. This is a proactive word. It implies taking responsibility for the creation of something. It is also a building word. When I determine to work out of an EMBER paradigm, I accept responsibility as an initiator and I become a builder.

M stands for Mutually. Mutually is a word which ties me to others, that there will be a joining with and interdependency with others. It connotes that I do not act alone, but in relationship with others.

B stands for Beneficial, and is tied to Mutually. Beneficial means for good, not evil. Mutual beneficence means what we do together will be good for both of us, not only good for me. A great example from Scripture would be Jeremiah 29:11 where God says, "For I know the plans that I have for you, declares the Lord, plans to prosper you and not to harm you, plans to give you a hope and a future."

E stands for Empathic, and it comes from the word empathy. Empathy is the ability to understand how another person feels, to "walk a mile in their moccasins." It is different from sympathy, a word it is often confused with. Empathy implies understanding, whereas sympathy implies agreement or the sharing of a feeling. Thinking empathetically takes effort and a commitment to setting our own agenda aside long enough to put ourselves in the other person's shoes. We need Christ to do this consistently. It was Jesus who, "although He was God, did not count equality with God a thing to be grasped, but emptied Himself, taking the form of a servant. . ."(Philippians 2:6-7) In our acronym, Empathic is tied to our final letter, R.

R stands for Relationships ... the key to all of life. In fact, our lives might be defined by the sum total of our relationships with God and man. Business, family, and our social life are each a collection of interdependent relationships. Empathic relationships are relationships based on an understanding of the other's needs, wants, position, etc. They are very Golden Rule oriented.

So what is EMBER really saying to us in terms of a commitment to a way of dealing with others effectively? Basically this: EMBER leaders commit that—insofar as it is in their ability to initiate and influence—they will strive to build relationships that are good for all parties and based on an understanding of the other person's desires and position.

Effective leaders gain strength from their understanding of the ones they lead. Many of us make little effort to understand where another is coming from before we try to solve all their problems or impose our wisdom on their dilemma. It is natural, and we can be leaders who don't listen or care about understanding. We can even succeed without applying EARS or EMBER, but we can never be as successful as we should be.

Let's turn the tables on ourselves again with the Golden Rule. If we could choose a leader who, by his/her actions, showed no understanding or concern for our point of view or position, or a leader who would take time to listen with the purpose of understanding us, with a commitment to treat us in a manner based on mutual benefit or no deal, which would we choose? It's totally obvious, isn't it? We, and those we lead, would all prefer to follow leaders who demonstrate genuine concern and respect for us as individuals. We often function under positional authority, but we never give it all we have to give. Given the chance, we would leave it in a heartbeat to follow a leader who treats us as valuable EMBER practitioners.

On Your Own

1. Rate yourself on a scale of 1–10. Are you a good listener?

2. Ask the same question of four people who are close to you and whom you trust to be honest to rate you.

3. Compare their answers to yours.

4. If your rating is not what you think it should be, try EARS for a month. Ask them to rate you again.

5. Think carefully about EMBER, and apply it to the key relationships of your life and how you perceive them. Are they mutually beneficial?

* *The Wilson Learning Institute*

Step 6: 2+2 Can =5 or 6 or 7

Though one may be overpowered by another, two can withstand him. And a threefold cord is not quickly broken.—*Ecclesiastics 4:12*

It is exciting to see the secular world embrace a biblical principle, even when they are unaware of its origin. The fact is all of the principles man has discovered which work and produce long-term success in relationships—(and what is business if not interconnected and interdependent relationships?)—are biblical principles ... albeit they are not articulated as such. The fact that man has a problem giving God credit doesn't change the source. God's ways applied to relationships are always best.

An example of this principle is our sixth step: "2+2 can = 5 or 6 or 7." This step focuses on the benefits of realizing the sum of the whole is greater than the total of the parts ... or many disparate parts working interdependently with synergy.

Synergy is different from compromise, although many of us confuse the two. Get this: Compromise says that in order for us to work together we must each give up a little of ourselves in order to cooperate. In a relationship of compromise, $1 + 1=1\frac{3}{4}$, really. Each is diminished by what he gives up to compromise, so the total will always be less than the sum of the parts.

Synergy says that we are mutually strengthened when our differences are added to our similarities. In a synergistic relationship, $1+1=3$, or maybe 4, or 5. For most of us, this is a radical concept since we have been trained more in the compromise mode of thinking.

Most of us think great leadership is getting others to think and act like we do, making them into little clones, as it were. The reason we think this way is we've been taught by people who also think that way. This inefficient paradigm has been the predominant view for a long time. Most leadership thinking over the last several hundred years was based on a military model called "command and control." Command and control is authoritarian and requires that all orders come down from the top of the organizational structure. Those who function below must conform. There is very little opportunity for innovation, creativity, or the unique expression of individualism. Through the years our military, educational system, and most of our businesses have functioned primarily under the command-and-control model. It works well in some situations, but not all. We obviously need structure, but not structure based on authoritarianism.

In the leadership continuum, there are two extremes. On one end is authoritarian leadership, which in its most evil expressions produces dictators and tyrants. They hold authority through power and force, such as Hitler and Stalin, who were the worst of this type of leader.

On the other end is relational leadership, which produces volunteer followers. Relational leaders do not need power to force others to follow them. They are followed voluntarily. Jesus Christ is the greatest example of a relational leader. The world sees Gandhi as another. All leaders fall somewhere along the continuum between authoritarian and relational leadership.

Likewise, all organizations will fit somewhere on a continuum between total structure and total freedom. Total structure means total control and command, and total freedom means anarchy, when everyone does their own thing. In the most effective organizations there is structure enough to assure efficient function, and freedom enough to maximize creativity and innovation. God has designed His Church as an illustration of how this blend works best.

First, God made everyone different. He never intended to have cookie-cutter children. He chose to give each of us different packages of gifts, talents, and abilities. We have different skills, education, genders, ages, cultures, and so on. It's not an accident; He means for it to be so. There is really only one commonality among His children; we all are one in His Son Jesus Christ. Jesus is our common Lord and our older brother, and God calls us the Body of Christ. The Body of Christ is God's business.

Within the Body of Christ there are those with different spiritual gifts (found in the Bible, primarily in 1 Corinthians 12 and Romans 12). He picked out what those gifts were to be, and gave them to us for the benefit of all of our brothers and sisters. It is interesting to note that He never gave a spiritual gift to any of us for our own benefit, but so His Body will be made stronger through the benefit for others as we use that gift. (1Corinthians 12:4–7)

God also gives us talents and abilities to complement the gifts He gave, and then combines them into offices, ministries, and functions within the Body. Then He places us where we can help most. (1Corinthians 12:18) God is specific to tell us that one gift, talent, or office is not more important than another; His Body will work best only when all the parts work together as they are designed. If even one part should decide (or be forced) to try to be just like another, to that degree the Body will not be all it can be.

God designed a structure for His Body so it can function in an orderly way, and of course Jesus is the CEO. He has appointed apostles, prophets, teachers, pastors, and evangelists to lead the various work groups He needs to get His product to the customers. Each of us is assigned to one of the work groups where we are to diligently use our gifts and talents. When we all work as designed, we don't need much supervision. But we all have an internal beeper, His Holy Spirit, just in case. His Body is designed to work best as an interdependent sum of the parts.

We don't want to take this analogy too far, and certainly mean no disrespect by comparing the holy design of God's work on earth to the ideal design of a business. But there is too great a parallel to ignore and principles too rich to be denied.

While there is structure within God's design for the Body of Christ, it is not so much as to inhibit the function of the individuality He created in each part. There is freedom to be all He designed us to be. But it is not freedom for anything we want; it is freedom as privilege. There is an ultimate authority in the Body of Christ, but that authority chooses to release to us all the uniqueness we are designed to be, rather than restrict us to sameness. Such authority allows our differences to add strength, to be synergistically complementary, so the sum of the whole is far greater than the total of its parts.

We don't see the Body of Christ working much as it is designed to work in our current church culture. Men have built authoritarian structures designed to serve their needs for command and control, rather than serve the customer's need for God in their life. We see a structure that tries to hold all of the "important" work in the hands of the top authority, leaving the rest of us to mill around, paying them to do God's work. It isn't working very well.

In our businesses, we have the same problem as the church. We try to work from the top down too much, without using the gifts and talents God placed in our teams. We are overly influenced by the command-and-control model and mind-set, so we don't seek synergy. Instead, we look for conformity. We are conditioned to think this way.

Our hope in the C12 Group is to prevent mediocrity and strive toward greatness in Christ. Remember, we said that effectiveness as a Christian leader means influencing others for Christ in the most powerful way possible. We will only be truly effective in this with volunteer followers. We will gather volunteer followers effectively only when we facilitate their freedom to become all they are designed to be, and when leading them to a higher purpose by encouraging them to grow.

A certain vulnerability comes with practicing synergy and empowering others to be all they can be. It means the release of some controls we think we have, recognizing that others may be even more talented or gifted in some areas than we are. There is a requisite humility to leading others into relationships that are designed to facilitate synergy. We are not alone in the struggle because it is natural to resist this kind of servant leadership. It fits with the teaching of Jesus when He said, "He who would be greatest among you must be the servant of all."(Matthew 20:26) It's not unusual for our nature to rebel against what appears to be a paradox in Scripture, and we all suffer from this reaction. It is in our nature. Whenever we depart from God's highest and best—be it in design or in practice—we diminish the potential of our results. Can we lead from command and control? Of course we can. Most do now, and it often works better than no control at all. The question isn't whether it will work, but whether it is the best. And the answer is always, "No, it is not God's best." If it were, He Himself would use it.

God doesn't use command and control, even though He could. He doesn't want mindless robots working by rote. He leads through love and expressions of uniqueness. Can we learn to do likewise?

As this concept applies to our ministries and our businesses, God has given us team members who have gifts different from our own. We may have the gift of evangelism, for instance, but our team members may have other gifts, such as giving or teaching. It is important for us to express our gifts through our business, but in the big picture it is perhaps more important to release our team to use and express their own gifts. We can do only so much ourselves. To be all that we can as a company for Christ, all must work together as He designed us. We inhibit and quench the Spirit when we try to get others to be like we are. We release the Spirit when we release them to be all He designed them to be: free to minister their gifts in the unique package He gave them.

There is more than enough room for all of us to be what God has designed us to be. In an ideal Christian business, the evangelists would lead people to Christ. The teachers would encourage and train others to grow in their faith. The administrators would keep things in order. Those with the gift of hospitality would welcome strangers and visitors. Givers would seek those who need help. Pastors would counsel and comfort the hurting. Exhorters would cheer everyone on, and the unbelievers would watch it all with their mouths hanging open. What a sight that would be! All the while, every one of them would continue to function as salespeople, secretaries, shipping clerks, vice-presidents, or crew chiefs. The synergy of the Spirit of God is incredible.

Can this really happen? Can we truly aspire to ministry in our business to this degree? Let's ask the reverse. If it is God's business and the gifts in each member of the team are there by His design, given to build up and edify His Body, how can it not be possible? Would He ask us to hide them under a bushel? Would He limit them to use only on Sundays in church? Not likely.

The local church will never be all that it is designed to be when it is led by a pastor who tries to do all the work of ministry by himself. By not releasing members to do the work of ministry according to their gifts, the church will continue to suffer. So it is with our businesses; the ministry in and through them will be less than they could be if we, as leaders, do the same. Ministry and productivity of all kinds are multiplied as those with potential are released. As such, they can make the greatest contribution in the context of the creative packages of gifts and talents given to them by God. We, as leaders, are called to do just that: to identify and release potential. Understanding the value and reality of synergy helps us immensely.

On Your Own

1. Reread the descriptions of relational leadership and authoritarian leadership in our segment. Then on the continuum of leadership below, mark your leadership style where you feel it falls.

   Authoritarian 5...4...3...2...1...X...1...2...3...4...5 Relational

2. Spend some quiet time to reflect on whether or not your ministry, and the ministry of your team, might be increased by a move in one direction or the other.

3. List three things you could do to accomplish a change, if needed.

4. On your organization chart, list the spiritual gifts and primary talents for each of your team members.

5. Ask yourself, "What is being done, or could be done, to more fully release each of them to more effective use of these gifts and talents?"

   Ask God for wisdom to release each to be all He designed them to be.

   If this proves beneficial to you, lead your team members to do the same where appropriate.

Step 7: Renew Daily and Finish Strong!

We sow a thought and reap an act, we sow an act and reap a habit, we sow a habit and reap a character, we sow a character and reap a destiny.—W. M. Thackeray

A man walking through the woods one day came across another man struggling to cut down a large tree with a saw. The first man stopped to watch, while the man strained and sweated. After a few minutes the man observed, "You need to sharpen your saw." "I can't," panted the second. "Can't you see I'm too busy cutting down this tree?"

If "Accept Personal Responsibility" is the foundational step, the seventh step, "Renew Daily and Finish Strong!" is the overarching one.

Recall that to be proactive is to accept responsibility for the initiation of positive action in the areas of life over which we have control. An effective person is a proactive person, a doer, a driver. In all seven steps, there is a requisite bias toward personal discipline and directed effort.

So the first three steps have to do with our inner selves; they deal with our efforts to direct our personal lives in the most positive manner possible. The second three have to do with how we relate most effectively with others, by creating and sustaining mutually beneficial interdependent relationships.

The seventh step is the wellspring: the strength and direction for the first six steps. It is the step of personal renewal and development.

Our effectiveness in the first six is hugely influenced by our understanding and application of the seventh.

1 Thessalonians 5:23 shows we are three-part people, each of us having body, soul, and spirit. For maximal effectiveness, each must be maintained in the highest state of usefulness and in the best shape possible. After all, we are the only "us" there are. We have only one pass at this life, one chance to get it right. Pro-activity begins with a commitment to care for ourselves and to control those things we can for the care of our body, soul, and spirit, pro-actively.

For instance, the Lord tells us through Paul the Apostle in 1 Corinthians 3:16 that our body is "the temple of the Holy Spirit:" a physical container we use to carry Him around. That means we are responsible to pro-actively care for our bodies. How we feel physically doesn't control our spiritual life, but it does influence it. For each of us there is a balance of diet, rest, and exercise that will keep our bodies in sufficient condition to do the things God has planned for our lives as leaders. No one else can take care of our bodies for us, or force us to ignore the responsibility for them. We must accept the responsibility for ourselves and maintain basic physical fitness.

What is basic fitness? In one sense it is whatever God tells you it needs to be, and there are exceptions based on individual differences. Subjectively, it would seem to be: keeping our weight within five to eight percent of what is recommended for our height, age, and build. That might include strength enough for 25 push-ups, 50 sit-ups, and to run two miles in less than 30 minutes, at a minimum. Proper diet, exercise, and rest make these criteria very reasonable.

Does this mean if we neglect the care of our physical body that we can't be an effective leader? No, it doesn't. But it means if we operate at less than our minimum level of basic fitness or our body breaks down before it should, we will not likely be as effective as we could be.

Many of us are like that man cutting down the tree. We think we are too busy to take the time to restore or renew the tools we need to be effective. Consequently, we struggle much harder and accomplish less than we could. Caring for our bodies is basic to our effectiveness. Paul said, "I discipline my body and bring it into subjection, lest, when I have preached to others, I myself should become disqualified." (1 Corinthians 9:27) As Christian leaders desiring to be as effective as we can, we can't overlook any area that can influence our success in the ministry God has designed us to fulfill. Keeping the container in good condition is basic. We really can't not have the time for it.

In addition to our body, our mind/intellect needs renewal and building up. Just as regular exercise strengthens and renews our physical self, regular use and exercise stimulates and enlarges our mental capacities. Too many of us quit learning when we leave school, if not before. Effective leaders are lifetime learners.

One of the basic requirements those who would be volunteer followers ask leaders is to lead them with competence. In other words, we demonstrate to them that we are growing and learning, and leading them to do the same.

Earl Nightingale, the noted trainer and motivator, challenged his students to spend five minutes each day studying something about their business or profession. He promised if this habit was applied for five years, anyone doing so would become a recognized expert in his/her field. Experience proves his theory: the author was a student of Mr. Nightengale's and has applied his theory for over 40 years.

In terms of ministry and our businesses, five minutes each day studying methods for increasing the scope and effectiveness of the ministry would pay enormous dividends in eternal fruit. Another five minutes spent in study relevant to the business itself, such as technology, would pay back big-time as well. Incremental learning is effective and always leads to an advantage. Why? Because very few bother to do it. Most leaders look for quick-fix solutions and easy answers, and very few are willing to feed their minds on a regular, systematic basis.

Five minutes each day devoted to reading, watching, or listening to a tape about your ministry and your business isn't much on the surface, but it is more than 99 percent of what the rest of people do. If effectiveness is our goal, how can we ignore such a simple thing? Proverbs 22:29 says: "Do you see a man who excels in his work? He will stand before kings; He will not stand before obscure men." Learning and growing in knowledge will strengthen our platform and help us to lead and influence others effectively.

Again, who can study and learn for me? No one. I must be proactive and do it myself. If my mental saw is to be sharp, I must take the time to sharpen it.

Of course we as Christians can train our bodies to marathon readiness and study to become intellectual giants, but if we stop there, we will still miss effectiveness by the definitions found in this book. Remember, we are looking at maximum effectiveness as a Christian leader, and define it as influencing others for Christ in the most powerful way possible. We can never do that if we are starving our own spirit.

What does it mean to starve the spirit? It means to ignore it or deny what it needs to grow and remain healthy. I can only grow and be healthy in the spiritual dimension of my life by growing in my relationship with my Father in heaven. Spiritual life is not a static achievement; it is a living relationship with the living God. If you remember our discussion in Step 1, we said since God has already made provision for me to be all He has designed me to be, and for me to have everything I need to be and do all He wants me to be or do, that my spiritual condition is really all up to me. It isn't up to Him. If it were, it would be perfect. I must choose to sharpen my saw spiritually as well as physically and mentally.

2 Timothy 2:15 says to "Study (or be diligent) to show yourself approved to God, a worker who does not need to be ashamed, rightly dividing the word of truth." Study. Be diligent. Pro-actively take in the word of truth. We can never be successful or effective as a

Christian leader without a growing relationship with God, founded on His Word. The testimony of every great Christian saint attests to this fact. Without exception, great Christian leaders have always been men and women who know God and know His Word. First Timothy 4:8 tells us, "… godliness is profitable for all things, having promise of the life that now is and of that which is to come." Godliness grows through knowing God and knowing His Word.

As with bodily training and mental study, spiritual development also takes time. That's what sharpening the saw is all about. The man in our story was too busy doing "hard" work to take the time to do "smart" work. Too many of us are like him when it comes to the spiritual dimension of our lives. We have time for everything else: social things, fun things, sport things, and, especially, business things. Most Christian business owners don't exercise or have a quiet time. Of those who do, almost all spend more time on the exercise than in quiet time. It is common to see a man spend an hour working out his body and maybe 15–30 minutes, if at all, praying, reading the Bible, or quietly listening for God.

What would happen to you and me if we reversed the ratios and started to spend two minutes with God for every minute we spend working out or studying business improvement technology? It would be an improvement, for sure, but in eternity it would prove to be a paltry investment. In fact, all of us will probably regret not spending more time with God when we had the chance. Someday, not too long from today, the condition of our bodies will be irrelevant, and how much we know about how to make a fortune making widgets won't mean anything at all. Everything that will matter to us will have come out of our relationship of understanding the will and way of God, and our obedience to Him.

Do you know what the problem is? The problem for us is we don't really believe we will die and go to heaven. We believe we'll live on just as we are and things will always be as they are now. If this were not true, we would see a different picture when we look at our lives. You see, we live out what we really believe to be true. If we really believed 1 Corinthians 3:11–15, and knew we are going to die and have our works judged by Jesus, and the results of His judgment will be with us forever, we would live very different lives.

Were that not true, we would live with the priority of eternal life, investing our time and money in eternal things first. We would be sure to feed our spirit. We would take time—all the time needed—to know God, learning to hear His voice, learning to love Him and how to please Him. We would make our physical and mental lives fit into our spiritual disciplines rather than vice-versa. But we don't live that way—at least most of us don't. We try to fit our spirituality in among all the other activities of life, most often giving it the last of our time, if any.

Most Christian business owners, or Christians in general, rush out of bed in the morning and dash to work without spending one moment with our Lord. Instead, they spend the whole day trying to scrape a little more mammon from the world, then return home too late and too tired to slip in a prayer at bedtime. Then they get up the next morning and do it all over again. Most Christians are so busy and over-committed doing "things," that finding time for God is impossible for them. It is only impossible because the things are more important than God. We don't really believe it will make a difference—at least that is what our actions imply. This is the primary reason that, unless we change our paradigm, we will live and die ineffectively as Christians. We are living as though there is all the time in the world to grow spiritually and do what God has planned for us.

Friends, we don't live here! If you are a Christian, this is not your home. Your home is in heaven, with Christ. You and I are pilgrims, temporarily on earth as Ambassadors for Christ. The Bible says, "God was in Christ, reconciling the world to Himself." (2 Corinthians 5:19) He has given us the ministry of reconciliation as Ambassadors for Christ. This is our true identity and our destiny. It makes no difference if we are the CEO of a huge company or the janitor. Our titles are not important and our position in the world doesn't matter. We are here on a journey. We had a specific beginning on the day of our birth, and have a specific end on the day of our death. That's when we go home. Every tick of the clock—every hour of every day—brings us closer to the promised judgment and final accounting of the effectiveness of our use of the time we are given. In the end, our eternity will be influenced by our commitment to this truth.

And here is another truth: For effectiveness to be real, it must be measured against an objective standard. At the Bema, our effectiveness as Christian leaders will be measured by the eternal fruit produced through our lives versus the potential that we have been given. God produces the fruit, but He does it through our lives of obedience and service. Eternal fruit means lives influenced toward God in Christ. It is people being saved, sanctified, and served through us. We can't measure all the results on this side of Judgment Day, but we can measure our effort. A farmer can't know in advance the size of his crop, but he can know where he has planted seed.

Sharpening the saw spiritually and growing in these truths happen primarily in our daily quiet time: communion with God, reading His Word, and talking with Him. It is the foundation from which our spiritual lives develop. Then it is worked out as we experience our relationships with others every day. Without a daily time of sharpening the saw spiritually, our effectiveness will be diminished … but by how much, we will never know. We can never know—in this life, at least—the results of decisions we don't make, but our effectiveness will be lessened. There are many differences among the great and effective Christian leaders of our heritage, and there is one common denominator. They all had a significant daily quiet time with God in Christ. What is significant? At least one hour.

Where that time comes from will most likely materialize by exchanging some of the worthless activities in Quadrant #4 for those with higher eternal value. The discipline of daily quiet time is indeed the foundation for effectiveness as Christians, because everything of value in our lives now and for all eternity grows out of our relationship with our heavenly Father, and that relationship starts by spending time with Him. There are "Two Steps to Your Most Important Hour"* that have proven successful for hundreds of Christians over the years.

First, commit the first hour of your day to God. Get up an hour earlier each morning and sit with Him in a quiet place. Read His Word, speak to Him, listen for His voice, and pray. Read something to make you more effective in business and in ministry that will challenge you to grow in your faith.

Second, make that hour nonnegotiable. That's right. Live a 23-hour day doing whatever He tells you to do in the first hour. In reality, we all live our lives regulated by the first appointment of our day: we set our alarm clocks based on what time we have to get up and be at the office, the airport, a client's, or whatever. Develop the discipline of setting the alarm one hour earlier and spend it with the Source of all that is good ... the One who loves you more than any other and proved it. The One from whom all wisdom flows and whose promise is: "I know the thoughts that I think toward you," says the Lord, "thoughts of peace and not of evil, to give you a future and a hope." (Jeremiah 29:11). One thing is certain: You will never regret the time you spend with Him in this discipline. Also, you won't be one bit more tired at the end of the day. We are all tired at the end of every day, so measuring how tired is tired, is impossible. By contrast, the benefits of nurturing our relationship with God are all measurable, both now and in eternity. Nothing in our lives is more important than nurturing our relationship with our Father! Everything that is truly important and valuable in this life and the life to come is built on this foundation. That is the testimony of every great Christian hero.

Finally, start keeping a daily journal of your thoughts and experiences gained during your quiet time. Take note of the scripture insights you want to remember or memorize. Record prayers prayed, God's answers, lessons from books you are reading, and anything else of importance to you. Writing things down helps us remember, and gives us a record to refer to at a later date. Examples of a successful quiet time journaling practice used by your author can be seen in the video, "Two Steps to Your Most Important Hour." It can be accessed on the C12 channel on You Tube. Watching it might be the best 43-minute investment you make this year!

So there we have it: Seven steps on a Christian road less traveled, to become highly effective Christians. The road begins with accepting responsibility for taking control of our lives to the extent that we can influence or control them, then deciding what things are most important to us and prioritizing our lives to accomplish them, and ending with a continuing development and maintenance program based on the truth of God's Word. You know we can't break God's truths; we can only obey and flow with them, or be broken by them. God has called us, saved us, adopted us as sons and daughters, provided His written Word to guide us, given His Spirit to empower and guide us, assigned work that is precious to Him, and even created a system of rewards. The rest is up to you and me. There is great power and potential available to each of us in accepting and applying these seven steps, and we must accept responsibility to be proactive.

On Your Own

1. In a quiet time and place, assess your physical condition. Are you basically physically fit? If so, go on to #2. If not, write a list of where you are less fit than the description given in this segment. Next, write a program of remedial actions for each as needed. Be realistic. Give yourself time, but make the commitment to become fit.

2. Analyze the time you spend acquiring new knowledge—not only what applies to your business, but other areas of life and interests. Are you a learner? Do you regularly make an effort to learn new skills or information to increase your knowledge and ability to do what God has asked you to do in your relationship with Him? Your spouse, if you have one? Your children? Your profession? Your community and the world at large? If so, go on to #3. If not, write out a goal to learn something new in at least one of these areas on a regular basis.

3. Are you spending a daily quiet time with God? Do you know His Word as well as you must to do all He asks? Can you hear from Him? If so, wonderful! If not, when will you start? If your saw isn't as sharp as it should be, who will sharpen it for you?

   I encourage you to start tomorrow by spending the first 60 minutes of each day reading the Bible, memorizing a bit of it, praying, and asking God to tell you what He has in mind for the day. Then read something that will help you grow spiritually, something to help you learn more about the work God has given you. Sharpen your saw every day. It can never be too sharp!

"Two Steps to Your Most Important Hour" video is available on the C12 YouTube channel.

Made in the USA
Lexington, KY
08 November 2017